To Mara, with love from
Daddy and Nonna
—R.F. & D.J.N.

For Elouan
—M.M.

Text copyright © 2023 by Robert Furrow and Donna Jo Napoli
Jacket art and interior illustrations copyright © 2023 by Marc Martin

All rights reserved. Published in the United States by Random House Studio,
an imprint of Random House Children's Books, a division of Penguin Random House LLC, New York.

Random House Studio and the colophon are registered trademarks of Penguin Random House LLC.

Visit us on the Web! rhcbooks.com

Educators and librarians, for a variety of teaching tools, visit us at RHTeachersLibrarians.com

Library of Congress Cataloging-in-Publication Data is available upon request.
ISBN 978-0-593-38163-2 (trade)
ISBN 978-0-593-38164-9 (lib. bdg.)
ISBN 978-0-593-38166-3 (ebook)

The artwork was rendered in watercolor, pencil, and digital collage.
The text of this book is set in 19-point Weiss.
Interior design by Rachael Cole

MANUFACTURED IN CHINA
10 9 8 7 6 5 4 3 2
First Edition

we are STARLINGS

INSIDE THE MESMERIZING MAGIC OF A MURMURATION

written by
robert furrow & donna jo napoli

illustrated by
marc martin

RANDOM HOUSE STUDIO
NEW YORK

We are starlings.
This morning is chilly.
We are restless to leave
this cold place.

We take to the air and meet up with more starlings.

And more.
We fly
for days.

We are a giant flock now.
There are hundreds of us!

There are thousands of us!

There are millions of us!

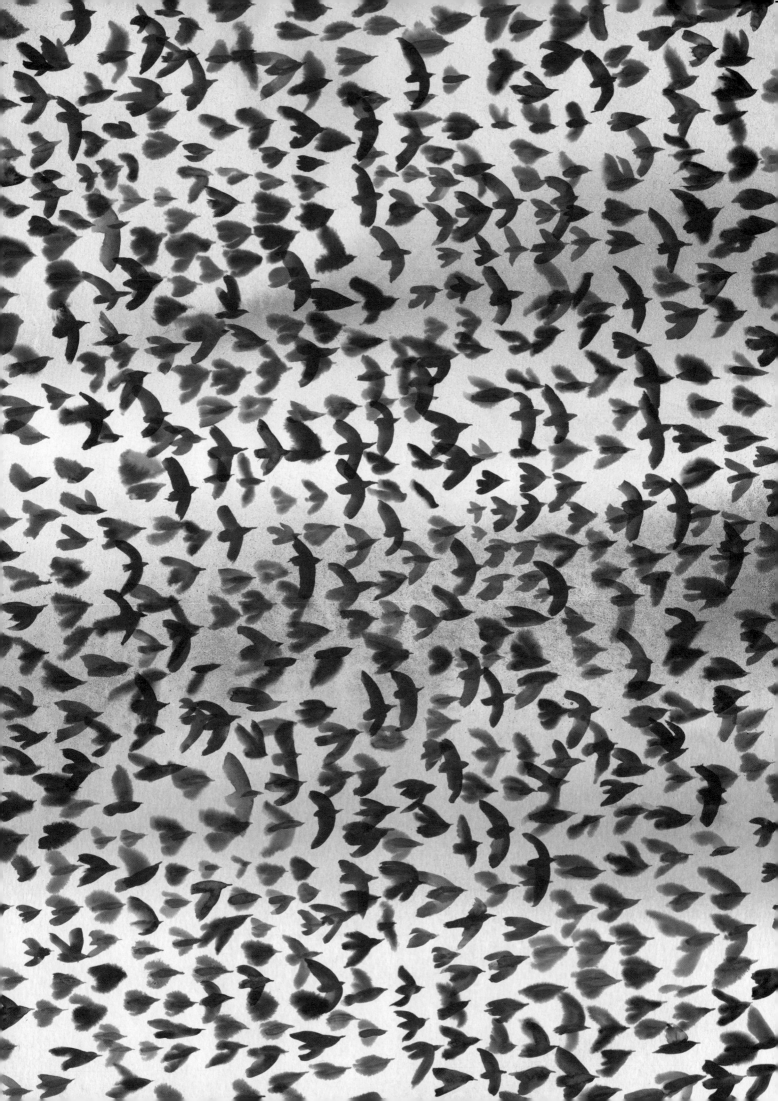

We fly, all of us together.

We flap flap our wings,
making a murmur even those
on the ground can hear.

We have become a murmuration of starlings.

We find strength and safety in numbers.
We find warmth in numbers.

We pay attention to the birds nearest to us. We are allies.
Our allies each have their own allies. We all guide each other.

Oh no!
A peregrine falcon!
We must get away!

I veer.

My allies veer.

Their allies veer.

We all change course.

Different birds fly closer now.

We make new allies.

We swirl and swirl.

The peregrine falcon
can't target any one of us.

We dance.

We twist through the sky like giant snakes.

Or fan out like humongous wings.

We loop back over ourselves in figure eights.

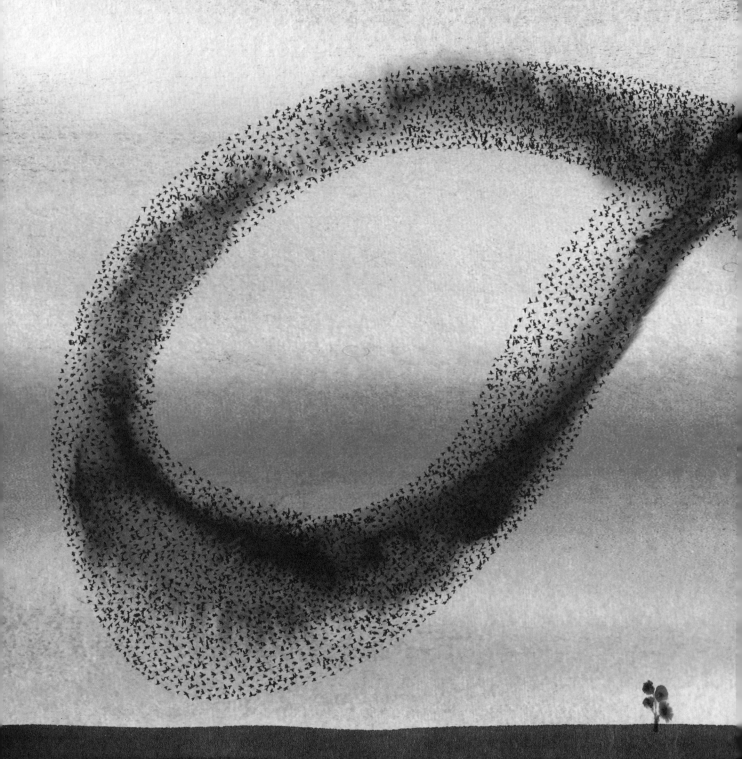

Goodbye, falcon!
The falcon flies off, defeated.

Then we land all at once.

And dance.

And dance.

We fly on in peace.

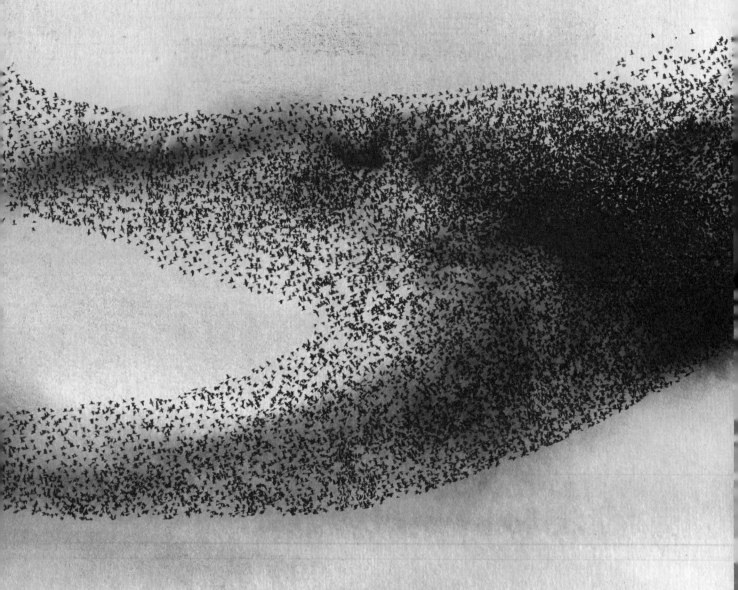

And now we are ready for fun.

That's our way—a sudden plop
to earth—the starling way.

We feed and roost.
We relax in the warmth of
so many hearts beating together.

We are starlings.

MORE ABOUT STARLINGS

The European starling (*Sturnus vulgaris*) originated in Europe, North Africa, and Asia, but now has populations throughout the world. The song of the starling is a jumble of whistles, clicks, squeaks, and pops. They are adept mimics, which means they can learn to imitate the sounds they hear. When a starling sings, you might hear it imitate a cat, a frog, a bird, or even a creaking door. In this story, though, the noise we find— the murmur—is not made from the starlings' vocal tract but from their wings as they travel through the sky.

Starlings are social—they can be found in flocks at any time of year. These flocks may include millions of birds, but each bird is able to avoid crashing into others while it flies. Given the size of the flocks, that may seem like a feat of engineering, but, in fact, the task is handled at a strictly local level. A starling in flight pays attention to its closest neighbors, moving in the graceful coordination known as a murmuration. Flocks ripple, whirl, and wave as each bird works to stay close to a small number

of neighbors, often six or seven, which means that they may seamlessly change neighbors as they fly and dance together.

After migrating or searching for food in the daytime, these flocks will land together to form a roost—a place where the birds can settle for the night. Starlings may sleep in trees or fields, or use office buildings, bridges, or other large structures. After a night's sleep, the birds' iridescent feathers sparkle in the morning light before they take to the air again. They may split into many smaller flocks, each looking for food in different areas, but the groups often rejoin at night to roost in the warmth and safety of their huge numbers.

Animals that travel in groups have many ways of keeping track of one another. Watch the groups of animals you encounter— in the air, on the land, in the sea. You might discover beautiful and clever patterns in the ways animals stay safe together.